SALOONS, SHOOTOUTS, AND SPURS
The Wild West in the 1800s

DAILY LIFE IN AMERICA IN THE 1800s

SALOONS, SHOOTOUTS, AND SPURS
The Wild West in the 1800s

by
Kenneth McIntosh

Mason Crest Publishers

MASON CREST PUBLISHERS INC.
370 Reed Road
Broomall, Pennsylvania 19008
(866)MCP-BOOK (toll free)
www.masoncrest.com

First Printing
9 8 7 6 5 4 3 2 1

Library of Congress Cataloging-in-Publication Data

McIntosh, Kenneth, 1959–
    Saloons, shootouts, and spurs : the wild West in the 1800s / by Kenneth McIntosh.
        p. cm. — (Daily life in America in the 1800s)
    ISBN 978-1-4222-1789-4 (hardcover)   ISBN (series) 978-1-4222-1774-0
    ISBN 978-1-4222-1862-4 (pbk.)   ISBN (pbk series) 978-1-4222-1847-1
    1. West (U.S.)—History—19th century—Juvenile literature. 2. Frontier and pioneer life—West (U.S.)—Juvenile literature. I. Title.
    F591.M146 2011
    978'.02—dc22
                                    2010022518

Produced by Harding House Publishing Service, Inc.
www.hardinghousepages.com
Interior Design by MK Bassett-Harvey.
Cover design by Torque Advertising + Design.
Printed in USA by Bang Printing.

Contents

Introduction

History can too often seem a parade of distant figures whose lives have no connection to our own. It need not be this way, for if we explore the history of the games people play, the food they eat, the ways they transport themselves, how they worship and go to war—activities common to all generations—we close the gap between past and present. Since the 1960s, historians have learned vast amounts about daily life in earlier periods. This superb series brings us the fruits of that research, thereby making meaningful the lives of those who have gone before.

The authors' vivid, fascinating descriptions invite young readers to journey into a past that is simultaneously strange and familiar. The 1800s were different, but, because they experienced the beginnings of the same baffling modernity were are still dealing with today, they are also similar. This was the moment when millennia of agrarian existence gave way to a new urban, industrial era. Many of the things we take for granted, such as speed of transportation and communication, bewildered those who were the first to behold the steam train and the telegraph. Young readers will be interested to learn that growing up then was no less confusing and difficult then than it is now, that people were no more in agreement on matters of religion, marriage, and family then than they are now.

We are still working through the problems of modernity, such as environmental degradation, that people in the nineteenth century experienced for the first time. Because they met the challenges with admirable ingenuity, we can learn much from them. They left behind a treasure trove of alternative living arrangements, cultures, entertainments, technologies, even diets that are even more relevant today. Students cannot help but be intrigued, not just by the technological ingenuity of those times, but by the courage of people who forged new frontiers, experimented with ideas and social arrangements. They will be surprised by the degree to which young people were engaged in the great events of the time, and how women joined men in the great adventures of the day.

When history is viewed, as it is here, from the bottom up, it becomes clear just how much modern America owes to the genius of ordinary people, to the labor of slaves and immigrants, to women as well as men, to both young people and adults. Focused on home and family life, books in this series provide insight into how much of history is made within the intimate spaces of private life rather than in the remote precincts of public power. The 1800s were the era of the self-made man and women, but also of the self-made communities. The past offers us a plethora of heroes and heroines together with examples of extraordinary collective action from the Underground Railway to the creation of the American trade union movement. There is scarcely an immigrant or ethic organization in America today that does not trace its origins to the nineteenth century.

This series is exceptionally well illustrated. Students will be fascinated by the images of both rural and urban life; and they will be able to find people their own age in these marvelous depictions of play as well as work. History is best when it engages our imagination, draws us out of our own time into another era, allowing us to return to the present with new perspectives on ourselves. My first engagement with the history of daily life came in sixth grade when my teacher, Mrs. Polster, had us do special projects on the history of the nearby Erie Canal. For the first time, history became real to me. It has remained my passion and my compass ever since.

The value of this series is that it opens up a dialogue with a past that is by no means dead and gone but lives on in every dimension of our daily lives. When history texts focus exclusively on political events, they invariably produce a sense of distance. This series creates the opposite effect by encouraging students to see themselves in the flow of history. In revealing the degree to which people in the past made their own history, students are encouraged to imagine themselves as being history-makers in their own right. The realization that history is not something apart from ourselves, a parade that passes us by, but rather an ongoing pageant in which we are all participants, is both exhilarating and liberating, one that connects our present not just with the past but also to a future we are responsible for shaping.

—*Dr. John Gillis, Rutgers University Professor of History Emeritus*

1800

1800 The Library of Congress is established.

1801

1801 Thomas Jefferson is elected as the third President of the United States.

1803

1803 Louisiana Purchase—The United States purchases land from France and begins westward exploration.

1804

1804 Journey of Lewis and Clark—Lewis and Clark lead a team of explorers westward to the Columbia River in Oregon.

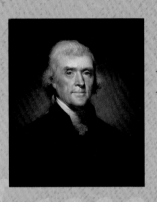

Time Line

1825

1825 The Erie Canal is completed—This allows direct transportation between the Great Lakes and the Atlantic Ocean.

1836

1836 On March 6, Mexican forces take the Alamo from Texas, after 13 days of siege.

1838

1838 Trail of Tears—General Winfield Scott and 7,000 troops force Cherokees to walk from Georgia to a reservation set up for them in Oklahoma (nearly 1,000 miles). Around 4,000 Native Americans die during the journey.

1812

1812 War of 1812—Fought between the United States and the United Kingdom.

1820

1820 Missouri Compromise—Agreement passes between pro-slavery and abolitionist groups, stating that all the Louisiana Purchase territory north of the southern boundary of Missouri (except for Missouri) will be free states, and the territory south of that line will be slave.

1823

1823 Monroe Doctrine—States that any efforts made by Europe to colonize or interfere with land owned by the United States will be viewed as aggression and require military intervention.

1839

1839 The first camera is patented by Louis Daguerre.

1844

1844 First public telegraph line in the world is opened—between Baltimore and Washington.

1847

1847 Brigham Young becomes president of the Church of Jesus Christ of Latter-day Saints.

1848

1848 Seneca Falls Convention—Feminist convention held for women's suffrage and equal legal rights.

1848(-58) California Gold Rush—Over 300,000 people flock to California in search of gold.

1854

1854 Kansas-Nebraska Act—States that each new state entering the country will decide for themselves whether or not to allow slavery. This goes directly against the terms agreed upon in the Missouri Compromise of 1820.

1856

1856 "The Life and Adventures of James P. Beckwourth" is published.

1861

1861(-65) Civil War —Fought between the Union and Confederate states.

1862

1862 Emancipation Proclamation—Lincoln states that all slaves in Union states are to be freed.

1862 The U.S. Congress passes the Homestead Act, designed to encourage families to move to the West.

Time Line

1876

1876 Alexander Graham Bell invents the telephone.

1877

1877 Great Railroad Strike—Often considered the country's first nationwide labor strike.

1878

1878 Thomas Edison patents the phonograph on February 19.

1878 Thomas Edison invents the light bulb on October 22.

1881

1881 Billy the Kid, or Henry McCarty, is killed on July 14 at 21 years of age.

1881 Shootout at the OK Corral in Tombstone, Arizona occurs on October 26.

1865   1867   1869   1870

1865 Thirteenth Amendment to the United States Constitution—Officially abolishes slavery across the country.

1867 United States purchases Alaska from Russia.

1865 President Abraham Lincoln is assassinated on April 15.

1869 Trans-continental Railroad completed on May 10.

1870 Fifteenth Amendment to the United States Constitution—Prohibits any citizen from being denied to vote based on their "race, color, or previous condition of servitude."

1870 Christmas is declared a national holiday.

of the 1800s

1882   1890   1893   1898

1882 Jesse James, an outlaw, gang leader, and bank/train robber, dies.

1890 Wounded Knee Massacre—Last battle in the American Indian Wars.

1893 Great Oklahoma land rush begins.

1898 The Spanish-American War—The United States gains control of Cuba, Puerto Rico, and the Philippines.

Part I
People of
the First Nations
and New Spain

Beginning in the 1830s, Americans referred to the lands beyond the Mississippi River as "the Wild West." This enormous region was "wild" in the sense that it was an unmapped wilderness—and untraveled Easterners imagined that the people living out West—Indians, fur trappers, and Spaniards—must be "wild" or uncivilized. (Ignorance often breeds prejudice!) When Anglo-Americans moved west, they actually encountered many well-developed societies that had been there for thousands of years.

The Blackfoot (who called themselves the Niitsitapi) were another Native tribe that lived in the American west, in what is now the state of Montana.

A Hogan, the traditional Navajo home.

More than 100,000 natives lived in California, hunting and gathering plant foods, fish, shellfish, and small game. They wove beautiful bark baskets and spoke many different languages. Northward up the Pacific Coast, other tribes lived in cedar-log homes, and traveled the waves in ornately decorated log canoes.

Further inland, the Diné (Navajo) lived in what is modern-day Arizona and New Mexico. They planted corn, and lived in circular homes called Hogans. They acquired horses and sheep from Europeans, and became expert riders and weavers. The Navajos excelled both in trade and in warfare, due to centuries of encounters with hostile Spaniards and competing tribes. The Ndee (Apache) were relatives of the Navajo, and shared many similar words and customs.

Pueblo Indians lived very differently from the Navajos and Apaches. Pueblo groups included the Hopi, Zuni, and other communities. They dwelt in permanent apartment-complex-like cities made of adobe bricks and plaster. They developed amazing ways to farm in the dry desert and followed a complicated calendar of ceremonial dances and rituals.

Further east on the Great Plains lived the buffalo hunters. These included the Oceti Sakowin (Sioux), Cheyenne, Numunuh (Comanche), and Apsaalooke (Crow). Superb horse riders, they hunted the vast herds of buffalo, and used every part of those beasts for food, clothing, and utensils. They lived in portable tepees, and frequently moved entire villages.

The Pueblo people lived in large communities made from adobe. In the twenty-first century, these are the oldest American cities still standing.

EYEWITNESS ACCOUNT

Native Buffalo Hunt

Francis Parkman came to West in 1846, when he was twenty-three years old, seeking to experience and write about the Plains Indians' way of life. Here, he describes a buffalo hunt:

With a bold and well trained horse the hunter may ride so close to the buffalo that as they gallop side by side he may reach over and touch him with his hand; nor is there much danger in this as long as the buffalo's strength and breath continue unabated; but when he becomes tired and can no longer run at ease, when his tongue lolls out and foam flies from his jaws, then the hunter had better keep at a more respectful distance; the distressed brute may turn upon him at any instant; and especially at the moment when he fires his gun.

The wounded buffalo springs at his enemy; the horse leaps violently aside; and then the hunter has need of a tenacious seat in the saddle, for if the buffalo throws him to the ground there is no hope for him. When he sees his attack defeated the buffalo resumes his flight, but if the shot be well directed he soon stops; for a few moments he stands still, then totters and falls heavily upon the prairie.

Throughout the nineteenth century, settlers moved onto Native lands, threatening their survival. Tribes alternated strategies—sometimes allying with the newcomers, other times fighting to defend themselves. The U.S. cavalry rounded up the Navajos and herded them from their lands into an internment camp, but later the Navajos managed to return and regain much of their ancestral territory. The Pueblo tribes held onto their cities through a careful balance of trade, treaty, and armed resistance. Some Native leaders, such as Geronimo, Crazy Horse, and Chief Joseph, became legends. Today, the First Nations of the West continue to practice their unique languages, arts, and spiritual ways.

The spiritual faith of the Native people of North America gave them courage and strength to survive.

Snapshot from the Past

A Vision of Troubles Ahead
(Southeastern New Mexico, 1823)

Red Antelope, a leader of his people, felt inwardly troubled, even though his tribe seemed at ease. For the past six months, the Numunuh (Comanche) had lived well, after making a treaty with the government in Mexico City. The treaty promised there would be no fighting or trespassing on Comanche lands. Since then, the young men had turned their thoughts from warfare to hunting, and as a result the People's bellies were full. Why, then, this sense of foreboding?

Red Antelope had set a meeting with Medicine Eagle, known to have strong puha—spiritual power. When they sat in Medicine Eagle's tepee, the seer spread out a pouch containing six freshly pulled peyote buttons.

Medicine Eagle pointed to the bundle and nodded to Red Antelope. "Chew these slowly." He passed a clay bowl filled with water to the war chief. "If your mouth feels dry, swish this around—but don't drink it. These will tell what you need to know."

Red Antelope nodded, and did as he was told. Soon, he was sweating, and the sacred designs painted on the inside of the tepee began to dance. He swished water in his mouth and vomited. And then . . . he felt as if he was flying in the air. High above the earth, Red Antelope looked down and saw all the villages of his people. He saw a black cloud that came from the South and rolled over their camps. From this cloud, he heard sounds of shouting, and gunfire and frightened screams. He understood that this cloud was the Mexican army, and they would soon break the treaty they had made.

Hours later, he awoke from his vision, feeling groggy but wiser. He now knew the reason for his unease.

When settlers from the Eastern United States moved into the Southwest, they came upon more than the Native tribes—they also encountered Hispanic settlements that were already hundreds of years old. From the time of Columbus until 1821, the Southwest was "New Spain."

Spanish religious workers had built a network of missions extending throughout the Southwest. These settlements had two aims: first, to convert Natives to the Catholic faith, and second, to produce wealth for Spain. In the missions, each Native resident owned two sets of clothes, and lived in small apartments, where they slept on buffalo-hide mattresses and cotton sheets. They farmed, raised cattle, and imitated European crafts. The heart of each mission was the church, and these were the most ornately decorated buildings of the Old West, with beautiful statues, carvings, and paintings depicting the Catholic faith. In some cases, the missions enabled Native people to live more comfortably than they would have outside; but on the other hand, diseases sometimes swept through the missions, killing entire communities of Native residents.

Outside the missions, Spanish settlers also farmed and raised cattle and sheep. They lived in multifamily compounds made of adobe that could serve as small forts. Families slept on mats

The Spanish built missions like this across the American West. The monks and nuns who lived here brought Christianity to the Native people.

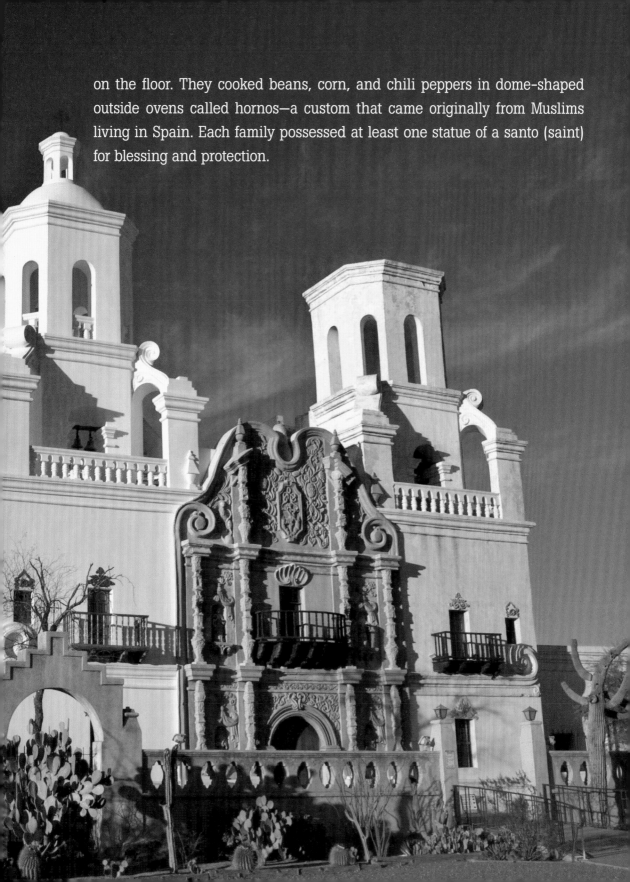

on the floor. They cooked beans, corn, and chili peppers in dome-shaped outside ovens called hornos—a custom that came originally from Muslims living in Spain. Each family possessed at least one statue of a santo (saint) for blessing and protection.

Spanish California was a prosperous region at this time. The Natives and Spaniards were on easy terms, disease was rare, and there was plenty of grass to raise cattle. Most settlers were rancheros (cattle farmers). Vaqueros (Spanish cowboys) wore stylish costumes and rode mustangs—descendants of Arabian steeds. Men and women

A Spanish Vaquero, or cowboy.

wore brightly colored clothes, and they enjoyed parties, dancing, and rodeo competitions to pass the time.

In the first half of the nineteenth century, the Southwest went through a momentous series of political changes. In 1821, Mexico separated from Spain, and so New Spain became New Mexico. Shortly after that, the Mexican gov-

The Battle of San Jacinto won Texas' independence from Mexico.

ernment encouraged Anglos to settle in Texas. Soon, Anglos outnumbered Hispanic Texans, and their cultures clashed.

On October 12, 1835, Texans revolted against Mexico, seeking to become an independent nation. On March 6, 1836 the Mexican army crushed Texan forces at the Alamo, but that defeat made the Texans so angry that they went on to victory at San Jacinto a month later. Texas joined the United States in 1845.

Two years later, the United States gained California and New Mexico as spoils of victory from the Mexican War. Today, the Southwest still retains many elements of its original Spanish language, religion, and culture.

EXTRA! EXTRA!
THE FALL OF THE ALAMO

The National Banner and Nashville Whig
March 29, 1836

On the 6th March about midnight the Alamo was assaulted by the whole force of the Mexican army commanded by Santa Anna in person, the battle was desperate until day light when only 7 men belonging to the Texan Garrison were found alive who cried for quarters, but were told that there was no mercy for them—they then continued fighting until the whole were butchered. One woman, Mrs. Dickson, and a Negro of Col. Travis were the only persons whose lives were spared. We regret to say that Col. David Crockett and companion . . . were among the number slain— Gen. Bowie was murdered in his bed sick and helpless. . . . The bodies of the slain were thrown into a mass in the centre of the Alamo and burned—the loss of the Mexicans in storming the place was not less than 1000 killed and mortally wounded.

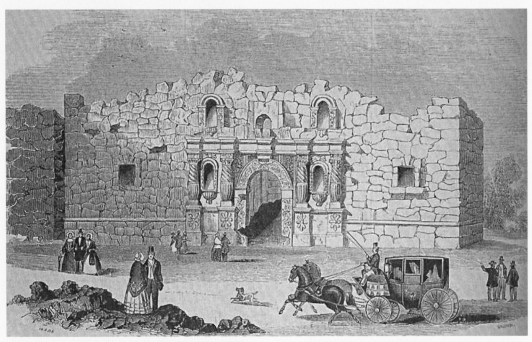

The Alamo mission as it looked in 1854.

Part II
Trappers and Miners

In 1803, the United States made the largest land deal in history by purchasing the Louisiana Territory from France, acquiring 828,000 square miles for 15 million dollars. At the time of sale, the French Foreign minister said, "You have made a noble bargain for yourselves and I suppose you will make the most of it."

The United States would indeed make the most of its bargain. But to do so, the government first needed to learn more about the land they had purchased: few English speakers had ventured into this Western territory, and it was almost completely uncharted. In order to map out the new land and explore its resources, Jefferson appointed Captains Meriwether Lewis and William Clark to lead an expedition from St. Louis to the Pacific Ocean and back.

Lewis and Clark Expedition

- Stops
- Preparation
- Recruitment
- Expedition Trail
- States

Captain Merryweather Lewis

members of the faculty at the University of Pennsylvania and gathered information about his proposed route.

Lewis chose William Clark to accompany him as co-leader of the expedition. Clark was a fellow Virginian with whom Lewis had served on the frontier in 1795. After Clark had spent several months studying astronomy and mapmaking, the two men were ready to set out on the adventure of their lives.

Meriweather Lewis, the official leader of the Lewis and Clark Expedition, was born to a Virginia planter family in 1774 and grew up to serve in the military. In 1801, he accepted an invitation from President Thomas Jefferson, an old family friend, to serve as his private secretary. The President soon set him a course of study that would equip him with the scientific skills he needed for the great expedition Jefferson had planned. Between 1801 and 1803, Lewis studied with

William Clark

The dangerous journey took more than two years to complete, two years of cold and rain, searing heat, sore feet, and heavy-laden backs. Despite the difficulties of the trip, only one member of the expedition died—and that was due to a ruptured appendix, not because of the dangers of the wild land. When Lewis and Clark returned they brought knowledge of travel routes, of plants and animals, and of the varied human inhabitants of the land.

Sacajawea played a major role in the success of the Lewis and Clark Expedition.

INCREDIBLE INDIVIDUAL
Sacajawea (1790–?)

This young Shoshone woman is famous because of her vital role on the Lewis and Clark Expedition. Sacajawea was the daughter of a Shoshone chief but another tribe kidnapped her when she was a little girl. Then, when she was a teenager, Toussaint Charbonneau, a French trapper, married her. In 1804, Lewis and Clark hired Charbonneau as an interpreter for their expedition, understanding that Sacajawea would also come along. Two months before the expedition left, she gave birth to her first child, a son named Jean. She carried her infant on a cradleboard as the group set out on their voyage.

When Lewis met the Shoshones, Sacajawea found that her older brother was now the chief. Sacajawea could have taken advantage of the situation to return to her people, but instead, she journeyed on with Lewis and Clark and her husband to the Pacific. On the return journey, Sacagawea and Charbonneau separated from Lewis and Clark at a Hidatsa village on the upper Missouri, and from this point they disappear from history.

Developers immediately recognized an important source of wealth in this newly purchased land—beaver pelts. Beaver fur has a natural tendency to clump together, or "felt," and it is waterproof. As a result, it made good hats.

In the early 1800s, all men wore hats. Popular styles were the Tricorn (what you might think of as a "pirate's hat") and the Stovepipe (think of Abraham Lincoln's hat). To manufacture all this headwear, hat makers needed more than 100,000 beaver pelts a year—and that many pelts could only be gained in the West. Merchants called the valuable pelts "hairy bank notes."

Prior to the Louisiana Purchase, French traders were already working in what they called New France. These were Voyageurs (travelers), also known as Courer Des Bois (runners of the woods). They sailed the Western waterways in birch bark canoes and traded goods to Natives in exchange for pelts. It was a rough life: Voyageurs often worked fourteen hour days and paddled their canoes at a speed of fifty-five strokes a minute. They carried 90-pound loads when they had to "portage" their canoes (walk the boats across land), and they often suffered from hernias. The waterways were treacherous and many Voyageurs drowned.

Some of the many styles of hat that were made from beaver fur.

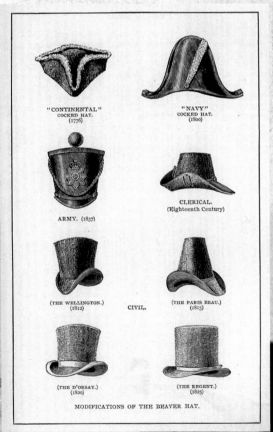

"CONTINENTAL" COCKED HAT. (1776)

"NAVY" COCKED HAT. (1800)

ARMY. (1837)

CLERICAL. (Eighteenth Century)

(THE WELLINGTON.) (1812)

CIVIL.

(THE PARIS BEAU.) (1815)

(THE D'ORSAY.) (1820)

(THE REGENT.) (1825)

MODIFICATIONS OF THE BEAVER HAT.

Fur Traders descending the Missouri in 1845.

Braving these hardships, the French traders played an important role in opening up the West. When English trappers moved into the West, they relied on the knowledge of the Voyageurs for survival.

Demand for beaver pelts resulted in competing fur companies. German-born immigrant John Jacob Astor formed one of the biggest, the American Fur Company, in 1808. Astor became so wealthy through this business that he loaned money to the United States government. Also in 1808, Manuel Lisa organized the Missouri Fur Company. Cuban-born Lisa was a demanding boss, but he had the courage, skill, and dogged ambition needed to succeed in the fur business. In 1822, another company joined the competition when Virginia-born ammunition manufacturer William Henry Ashley founded the Rocky Mountain Fur Company.

The French Voyageurs explored the waterways of the West in birch-bark canoes.

Jim Beckwourth was one of the most famous "Mountain Men."

Americans were so fascinated with his adventures that they were published in 1856 in a book titled *The Life and Adventures of James P. Beckwourth*. The stories were probably mostly fictional by the time they made it to print!

The fur companies relied on trappers—rugged individuals called "Mountain Men." These hardy souls survived in the wilderness by means of extraordinary stamina, survival skills, and familiarity with the Natives. They spent most of their time working traps in the mountain streams, traveling by horse and mule, hauling tepees to dwell in, dressing in skins, and eating berries and meat that they hunted. They interacted with people of the First Nations, trading goods and forming treaties. Many took Indian brides, and some

INCREDIBLE INDIVIDUAL
Jedediah Strong Smith (1799–1831)

When he was twenty-three years old, Jedediah Smith headed west carrying a butcher knife and a Bible. He was determined to trap beavers, make friends with the Indians, and make money in the process. Two years later, he survived a grizzly bear attack and then, at age twenty-six, he set the all-time record for the most beaver caught in a single season—668 pelts.

After that, the value of furs declined, so Smith set out to chart the unmapped wilderness.

This portrait of Jedediah Smith was drawn by a friend of his.

He was the first white man to travel across the Rocky Mountains to California, the first to cross the Great Salt Lake Desert, and first to travel overland from Southern California up to the Pacific Northwest. These treks were vital in establishing routes for later traders and settlers.

In May of 1831, a Comanche war party killed Smith but, though he worked in the West for only nine years, he lived on in legend. As one companion recalled, "Jed is half grizzly and half preacher."

became honorary tribal members. For example, Jim Beckwourth was born as a slave in the South, made his way west, worked as a fur trapper, and became a War Chief of the Apsaalooke (Crow) Tribe. In later years, when gold miners and then settlers moved west, the Mountain Men served as guides.

Gold!

In January 1848, John Sutter discovered gold at Coloma, California, and within two years, more than a quarter-million gold-hunters stampeded into California. These men, known as 49ers, worked hard to reach the Pacific Coast. Some braved the long and brutal trek by wagon across the plains and deserts.

Many travelers on the "prairie schooners" died; one outbreak of cholera in 1849 killed 5,000 passengers on the wagon trains. Other travelers, with more money, sailed around South America in newly-developed "clipper ships." One clipper captain boasted of making the trip from Boston to California in the "extreme" short time of ninety-one days. Most of the Gold Rush immigrants to California were male: in 1850, women comprised only 8 percent of Californians.

If you wanted to get to California's gold fields, passage on a clipper ship was one of your options.

Despite the rumors of gold nuggets lying on the ground, mining proved to be hard work. A miner could pan in the river, but most miners could only sift through fifty pans in a ten-hour day, and that produced barely enough gold to live on. Wooden sluices were more efficient, and tunneling also produced

A gold miner's life was hard and often disappointing.

more gold—but these methods required miners to form small companies that ate away at their profits. Miners worked in cold rivers and boiling summer heat, ate rations of sourdough, salt pork, and—when lucky—beans and dried apples. They suffered from aching muscles and bouts of illness. Most of them barely broke even, but hope lured each miner onward—maybe, just maybe, tomorrow he would find that one huge nugget worth thousands of dollars.

EXTRA! EXTRA! GOLD RUSH!

Donner Party Disaster
California Star

(In the winter of 1847 snow trapped a wagon train headed for California and the party ran out of food. Two brothers, Jacob and George Donner, were leaders of the group.)

After wandering about a number of days bewildered in the snow, their provisions gave out, and long hunger made it necessary to resort to that horrid recourse casting lots to see who should give up life, that their bodies might be used for food for the remainder. But at this time the weaker began to die which rendered it unnecessary to take life, and as they died the company went into camp and made meat of the dead bodies of their companions. After travelling thirty days, 7 out of the 16 arrived within 15 miles of Capt. Johnson's, the first house of the California settlements; and most singular to relate, all the females that started, 5 women came in safe, and but two of the men, and one of them was brought in on the back of an Indian. Nine of the men died and seven of them were eaten by their companions.

EYEWITNESS ACCOUNT

Vigilante Justice

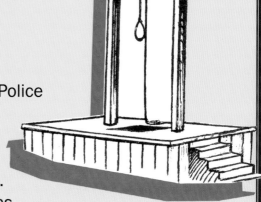

In 1849, the entire San Francisco Police Force abandoned their posts and went off to the gold fields, so miners had to act as vigilantes (take the law into their own hands). In 1851 Mrs. Louise Clapp wrote to her sister in Massachusetts and described the fate of a miner who was caught stealing gold.

The gallows were a common form of justice in the Wild West of the 1800s.

At one o'clock . . . the judge charged the jury, and gently insinuated that they could do no less than to bring in with their verdict of guilty a sentence of death! After a few minutes' absence, the twelve men, who had consented to burden their souls with a responsibility so fearful, returned, and the foreman handed to the judge a paper, from which he read the will of the people, as follows: That William Brown, convicted of stealing, etc., should, in one hour from that time, be hung by the neck until he was dead.

By the persuasions of some men more mildly disposed, they granted him a respite of three hours to prepare for his sudden entrance into eternity. He employed the time in writing, in his native language (he is a Swede), to some friends in Stockholm. God help them when that fatal post shall arrive, for, no doubt, he also, although a criminal, was fondly garnered in many a loving heart.

The execution was conducted by the jury, and was performed by throwing the cord, one end of which was attached to the neck of the prisoner, across the limb of a tree standing outside of the Rich Bar graveyard, when all who felt disposed to engage in so revolting a task lifted the poor wretch from the ground in the most awkward manner possible. . . . In truth, life was only crushed out of him by hauling the writhing body up and down, several times in succession, by the rope.

Snapshot from the Past

The Rendezvous, Wyoming's Green River Valley, 1837

Each year, representatives of the American Fur Company met their trappers out in the West, in order to exchange pelts for pay and goods. These annual gatherings were called "rendezvous."

Fourteen-year-old Henry Leary fled from apprenticeship to a blacksmith in St. Louis, and convinced the leader of a supply-wagon to take him on as a hired hand. The wagon headed into the wilderness, finally arriving in Wyoming, in June, at the mountain men's rendezvous.

The wagon master put Henry to work setting up large tents, but the young man just wanted to gawk at the sights. These fur trappers were the most uncivilized people he had ever laid eyes on. They wore buckskin leggings and jackets, with long fringe. Others wore brightly colored cotton shirts, or, in the colder morning, jackets made from red Hudson Bay blankets. They decorated their outfits randomly with "foofaraw": beads, feathers, skins, tails, or bones of various creatures. The trappers were a ragged and unkempt lot, smelling of smoke and sweat.

The first day of the rendezvous, the trappers all drank to excess, swapping a surprisingly large share of their years' pelts for whiskey that the company provided. They danced wildly, yelled and bragged and cussed. Some engaged in wrestling matches or—if they really had a bone to pick—in fisticuffs. Every few minutes, drunken trappers fired their rifles into the air. On the outskirts of the meeting ground, the Native wives of the trappers stood watching, chatting among themselves, pointing and giggling at their inebriated and unrestrained men folk.

Henry grinned to himself. "I am certainly in the Wild West now!"

These men and their two sons were trappers in the 1800s.

Typical trappers were flamboyant figures, a little like the bikers of today!

People from China first came to America during the California Gold Rush.

Some folks did make big money in the rush, but these were not miners: they were the entrepreneurs that miners contemptuously called "vultures." Wherever miners gathered, merchants made a brisk trade in shovels, picks, pots, kettles, mules, clothing and—especially—liquor. There was a joke that a pot of gold was worth a pot of beans—and that was only a slight exaggeration. Gambling was the most common pastime, and professional card sharks made a brisk trade. The few "fancy ladies" who ventured west were in great demand, exchanging their good reputations for quick wealth.

The California Gold Rush also beckoned Chinese immigrants to America. By 1853, more than 25,000 Chinese had arrived in San Francisco. The Anglo majority greeted these new immigrants with prejudice and discrimination, driving Chinese miners off gold-claim sites. The Chinese not only mined for gold, but worked as cooks, peddlers, and storekeepers, taking jobs nobody else wanted. In 1852, California required Chinese miners to pay a "foreign miners' tax" of $3 each month—at a time when the average Chinese miner made only $6 monthly. It was a rough beginning for Chinese immigrants, but they nonetheless managed to create communities in the West, leading to the rich cultural legacy of Chinese-Americans today.

Part III
Cowboys and Settlers

The Pioneers

Beginning in the 1840s, thousands of Americans traveled from the East to new territories in the West, seeking land where they could achieve their dreams. Promoters enticed migration by advertising Oregon and California as "the loveliest country on earth."

Most pioneers traveled by covered wagon. Oxen pulled the wagons; and since oxen cannot be controlled by

reins, the driver had to walk beside the beasts and guide them—clear across the country. Loaded goods filled the wagons, and that left room for only the elderly and the very young. Healthy pioneers—including women and older children—walked alongside.

Settlers called their wagons "prairie schooners," but it wasn't a very good comparison: unlike fast-traveling ocean vessels, these wooden vehicles traveled at the speed of only two miles per hour. Some pioneers were too poor to purchase a wagon, so they bought a "walking ticket" that allowed them to follow along with a wagon train—by foot, all the way. On average, pioneers took six months to cross the 2,000-mile Oregon Trail; and the journey was dangerous. Thirst, starvation, stampedes, and accidents were common threats.

Once they arrived, pioneers would "stake a claim" to land. In 1841, Oregon offered each settler 640 acres of land, plus 160 more for each wife and child. Then, the pioneer family needed shelter. At first, they could live in the wagon. That didn't offer much space, so the family would get to work on a log cabin or sod house.

It was hard work cutting trees, then squaring them, all with simple tools. Sod homes, made from squares of dirt, were more convenient to make on the Great Plains. Many settlers had jettisoned belongings to lighten their wagons, so they constructed new furniture by hand. Clothing also wore out on the long trek west, so pioneer families made new garments from tent cloth.

EYEWITNESS ACCOUNT

The Great Oklahoma Land Rush

In 1893, the United States Government offered 42,000 parcels of land for development in what had previously been "Indian Territory." The country was having hard times economically, so thousands lined up for a mad race across the border to claim lands. Seth Humphrey and his brother raced on their bicycles. Seth describes the scene:

It has been estimated that there were somewhere around one hundred thousand men in line on the Kansas border. Viewed from out in front the waiting line was a breath-taking sight. First in the line was a solid bank of horses; some had riders, some were hitched to gigs, buckboards, carts, and wagons, but to the eye there were only the two miles of tossing heads, shiny chests, and restless front legs of horses. While we stood, numb with looking, the rifles snapped and the line broke with a huge, crackling roar. That one thundering moment of horseflesh by the mile quivering in its first leap forward was a gift of the gods, and its like will never come again. The next instant we were in a crash of vehicles whizzing past us like a calamity.

It might sound romantic living in a log cabin, but the average pioneer home was smaller and cruder than you might imagine. An entire family—on average, two parents plus four children—lived in a single room the size of an average American living room today. The parents slept on the only actual bed, children slept on mattresses that were pulled out each evening. The women cooked on a crude fireplace or very small woodstove. Windows lacked glass: they were either wide open—letting flies in—or else covered with wooden shutters.

Settlers made their livings through a variety of pursuits. Wheat was a favorite crop. Cattle provided milk and meat, and chickens produced eggs to live on. Families supplemented their meals by hunting and fishing. Many settlers planted fruit trees. It was a hard life, but many pioneers were determined and resourceful, so they survived and began the villages and cities that still exist in the American West today.

A settler's first job was to plow the sod. He could then begin to plant his crops— and next, he could build a temporary home from the sod.

These settlers have built their barn, but they are still living in the sod house seen in the background on the right.

Eventually, settlers would build themselves wooden homes and get down to the business of raising children, farm animals, and crops.

The Cowboys

In 1862, Congress passed the Homestead Act, hoping that farming families would fill up the western territories. Unfortunately for their plans, the Great Plains states proved too difficult for farmers to live on. These regions were, however, very well suited to another sort of business: raising cattle. Big investors bought enormous tracts of land where they could graze cattle, then drive their herds to cattle towns such as Abilene or Dodge City, where the livestock were sold at a generous profit and shipped east. At the same time, many unemployed men were looking for work: Civil War veterans, unsuccessful farmers, new immigrants, and freed slaves jumped on the opportunities to herd cattle.

Cowboy life was rugged and demanding. The men had to put in long days "biting the dust," working outside in snow, rain, and desert heat, living off bacon and beans, roping and driving large herds of 1,000-pound Texas longhorns, and

Fortunately, the skills and technology for cowboy life were already in place. Hispanic Vaqueros (whom Anglo cowboys called "Buckaroos") had long ago trained their mustangs for ranching, and they had designed garments such as broad-brimmed hats and leather chaps needed for life on the range; furthermore, they had become artists with the lariat needed to control their herds. The "new-breed" cowboys of the later 1800s literally learned their ropes from these Vaqueros.

defending against rival ranchers and rustlers. Ranchers paid their workers an average of $25 a month, which was not much money, even by the standards of the 1870s. Most cowboys were in their teens or twenties; the work was too demanding for older men.

This nineteenth-century photograph shows the interior of the ranch house where cowboys spent their free time.

Railroads, Cities, and Gunfighters

In the mid-1800s, Americans faced a frustrating problem: how could people travel conveniently from the settled eastern states to the beckoning West? Developers dreamed of a railroad line connecting the two sides of the continent, and in 1862, the Union government began work on the transcontinental railroad. Two construction companies hired thousands of Chinese and Irish laborers; these workers endured dangerous conditions, rough weather and very low wages, but they got the job done.

On May 10, 1869, workers completed the first railroad connecting the two halves of the United States. The "Iron Horse" then quickly transformed the West as cities sprang up along the rails.

Before this, gold miners and cowboys had relied on vigilante justice.

The coming of the railroad changed America, especially the West.

They were rough-and-tumble men, comfortable with taking law into their own hands. However, as more families moved to the frontier, and as merchants established their businesses, citizens of the increasingly "civilized" West clamored for "by-the-book" law enforcement.

There were indeed unsavory and dangerous outlaws in the West at this time. Partly, this was due to the aftermath of the Civil War; bitter conflicts fought in Kansas and Missouri left angry and desperate men, well trained in horsemanship and dueling. At the same time, the lack of organized law made it easy for such men to live by robbery. The press romanticized some outlaws, such as Billy the Kid, Jesse James, and Butch Cassidy, although their actual deeds were selfish and violent.

Outlaw Jesse James and his brother Frank James were Confederate guerrilla fighters during the Civil War. They were accused of participating in atrocities committed against Union soldiers. After the war, as members of one gang or another, they robbed banks, stagecoaches, and trains. Despite popular portrayals of James as a Robin Hood who robbed from the rich and gave to the poor, there is no evidence that he and his gang used their robbery gains for anyone but themselves.

EXTRA! EXTRA!

Gun Fight at the OK Corral
Tombstone Epitaph

(History's most famous gunfight was the shootout at the OK Corral in Tombstone Arizona, on October 26, 1881. The Earp Brothers and friend Doc Holliday were on one side, representing the law, against the Clantons and McLowrys. Shortly after the fight, Wyatt Earp gave this statement in the newspaper.)

Virgil said, "Throw up your hands. I have come to disarm you." Billy Clanton and Frank McLowry commenced to draw their pistols. When I saw Billy and Frank draw their pistols I drew my pistol... I knew that Frank McLowry had the reputation of being a good shot and a dangerous man, and I aimed at Frank McLowry. The two first shots which were fired were fired by Billy Clanton and myself he; shot at me, and I shot at Frank McLowry... The fight then became general. My first shot struck Frank McLowry in the belly. He staggered off on the sidewalk but first fired one shot at me.

I never drew my pistol or made a motion to shoot until after Billy Clanton and Frank McLowry drew their pistols. When I went as deputy marshal to help disarm them and arrest them, I went as a part of my duty and under the direction of my brother the marshal. I did not intend to fight unless it became necessary in self defense, and in the performance of official duty. When Billy Clanton and Frank McLowry drew their pistols I knew it was a fight for life, and I drew and fired in defense of my own life and the lives of my brothers and Doc Holliday.

From the Civil War until 1900, the West was shaped by a new and deadly piece of technology—the Six-Shooter. Cowboys, miners, outlaws, and lawmen valued the revolver that had been invented by Samuel Colt and then copied by other manufacturers. Between 1866 and 1900, gunmen on both sides of the law shot and killed more than 20,000 people west of the Mississippi;

it was truly the age of the gun-fighter.

By the 1880s, most cities in the West hired lawmen to protect against outlaws. It wasn't easy to get "squeaky clean" gunmen, so, to quote Western historian R.L. Wilson, "The line separating lawman from criminal was sometimes faint." Lawmen such as Bat Masterson, Wyatt Earp, Pat Garrett, and Buckey O' Neill gained fame for their courage and marksmanship.

The Colt Six-Shooter allowed gunfighters to shoot more quickly and efficiently—which made them deadly.

The Peace Commissioners of Dodge City; Wyatt Earp is in the front row, the second from the left.

The end of the nineteenth century brought with it the end of Native freedom and independence in America—and yet the tribes managed to hold on to their identities and survive.

From History to Legend

In the last decades of the 1800s, the western territories became increasingly less wild as the government suppressed the freedoms of the First Nations people, as law increased, and as cities grew larger and more sophisticated. At the same time, the Wild West of history transformed into the fabled Wild West that still lives on today.

Throughout the 1800s, Native warriors resisted efforts to take their lands. The federal government broke numerous treaties, and pushed tribes onto smaller and smaller areas. On December 29, 1890, troops of the U.S. Seventh Cavalry equipped with four rapid-fire cannons, surrounded a camp of Lakota Indians near Wounded Knee Creek, South Dakota. Cornered, the Sioux agreed to turn themselves in to a nearby reservation. There was a scuffle between soldiers and Natives, and the Seventh Cavalry opened fire from all sides, killing men, women, and children, as well as some of their own fellow troopers. It was a tragic end to the Native struggles against forced location.

At the same time, law enforcement prevailed over the outlaws. The Wild Bunch was the last famous outlaw gang in the West. They rustled cattle, held-up banks, and robbed trains in the final years of the 1800s until, pursued by Pinkerton detectives, the gang split up. The most famous members—Butch Cassidy and the Sundance Kid—fled to South America, where they faded into history.

With the taming of the Wild West, the Sundance Kid and his pal Butch Cassidy disappeared from history.

The So-Called Cancer and Folk Medicine (Kansas Prairie, 1880)

Medical technology in the 1800s was frighteningly unscientific.

Twelve-year-old Sarah Cameron fretted by the door of the family's sod house, waiting for her father to return with Uncle Hiram. They had gone on the family's buckboard wagon to Dodge City, where there was an honest-to-goodness medical doctor, to get help with the scabs that had been forming on Uncle Hiram's skin.

"They're here!" Sarah called to her mother, who was busy plucking a chicken out back.

Her mother ran with her to meet the men. "Well?"

Uncle Hiram looked grim. "The doctor says it is cancer, and it will eat away at me until I die—and that will be soon."

Sarah's mother grew pensive. "Honey, go look for some of that weed they call sheep sorrel. And Jeb"—she said to her husband—"fetch gunpowder and open that last bottle of whiskey."

When the three ingredients were gathered, Mother asked Sarah to grind equal parts in a small mortar-and-pestle. The resulting medicine paste smelled awful, but under the circumstances, Uncle Hiram did not complain as Mother rubbed it on his skin.

A week later, his skin looked smooth as a baby's.

"Thank the Lord, it wasn't cancer after all," beamed Uncle Hiram.

"Just goes to show," Sarah replied, "doctors don't know everything."

INCREDIBLE INDIVIDUAL
Brigham Young (1801–1877)

No history of the West would be complete without including the Mormons (Latter Day Saints). In 1844 an Illinois mob killed the prophet and founder of their religion, Joseph Smith. That left thousands of believers bewildered over their future. Brigham Young was in many ways similar to Joseph Smith; he grew up in New York working as a farmer, carpenter and businessman. He was a devout believer in the Mormon faith, but also strongly practical. Young once said, "Prayer is good, but when baked potatoes, and pudding, and milk are needed, prayer will not take their place."

At a large meeting, the Latter Day Saints elected Young to succeed Smith as their prophet. He then ordered an audacious move across 1,400 miles of wilderness to the largely unknown land of Utah. Over the next three years, more than 16,000 Mormons followed Young across the country. Most went by wagon train, but 3,000 of the poorest made the trek on foot pulling hand carts. When the settlers arrived at Salt Lake Valley, Young declared "This is the place." Later, he wrote, "The Spirit of Light rested upon me and . . . I felt there the saints would find protection and safety."

With the passage of time, Western life became more like that of the eastern United States. In the cities, new settlers tore down rough wooden buildings and replaced them with classical brick structures and fancy Victorian homes. New train lines brought in goods and services at lower prices. Citizens of the booming western towns built churches and outlawed gambling and prostitution.

As the historical Wild West faded, one man found a way to transform its stories into enduring legends. "Buffalo Bill" Cody, who had served as a scout, hunter and soldier in the 1860s and 1870s, began his "Wild West Show" in 1883. This was a combination of theater and circus, featuring famous Western characters—both whites and Natives— re-enacting the feats of their younger

Buffalo Bill was a showman extraordinaire who helped keep the Wild West alive in the imaginations of people around the world.

years. The show was immensely successful, and toured the United States and Europe for more than a decade. Cody supported the rights of women and Native Americans, and he also promoted conservation of the American wilderness. At the same time, he brought the drama and excitement of the historical Wild West to thousands of enthralled onlookers.

Cody, along with others who dramatized the Wild West, ensured that its legends would be told and retold throughout the twentieth century and beyond. Even today, the Wild West lives on in the imaginations of people all around the world.

Frederic Remington, whose artwork has been used several times throughout this book, also kept the Wild West alive by recording it in paintings like this one. He wrote, "I knew the wild riders and the vacant land were about to vanish forever . . . and the more I considered the subject, the bigger the forever loomed. Without knowing how to do it, I began to record some facts around me, and the more I looked the more the panorama unfolded."

Think About It

The settling of the American West brought different groups of people together—Native Americans, the descendents of early Hispanic settlers, and Americans from the East—in various ways, but often in conflict. From the Battle of San Jacinto to the various "Indian Wars," it was eventually the "Anglo" culture of the Eastern United States that proved dominant.

- History is almost always written from the perspective of the "winning" side. How would you tell the story of the "Wild West" from the perspective of a Navajo tribesperson or a Hispanic vaquero?

- What do you think the West would be like today if it had been the Native Americans who ended up the winning side in the battle for dominance? What if it had been Hispanic people?

- Despite the "Anglo" defeat of Hispanic and Native powers in the 1800s West, the region today is a rich mix of these three cultures. What are some of the values and traditions of each of these three major cultural groups in the American West?

- How do these three cultures interact positively with each other, and how might they still be in conflict?

Words Used in This Book

allying: Uniting on the same side, often by official treaty.

audacious: Fearless and brave, without too much concern for any consequences.

chaps: Leather leggings worn over pants to protect a cowboy on horseback.

discrimination: Unfair treatment based on prejudice.

entrepreneurs: People who take the risk of starting new businesses and are committed to success.

First Nations: The Native People of North, Central, and South America, often called "Indians" or Native Americans.

hernias: Injuries to the abdominal region often caused by heavy lifting.

internment camp: A place where groups of people are held like prisoners, often in primitive conditions.

prejudice: Negative and hostile feelings, opinions, or attitudes, regarding a racial, religious, or national group.

romanticized: To have unrealistic, positive impressions of a time, place, or situation by concentrating on the best parts of it.

spoils: Possessions confiscated or stolen from the defeated by the winning side in warfare.

vigilante: Taking the law into your own hands and punishing criminals without proper legal procedures.

Find Out More

In Books

Brown, Dee. *Bury My Heart at Wounded Knee, Illustrated Edition: An Indian History of the American West.* New York: Sterling Publishing, 2009.

Bryant, Jill. *The Wagon Train.* Mankato, Minn.: Weigl Publishers, 2003.

Clayton, Lawrence, Jim Hoy, and Jerald Underwood. *Vaqueros, Cowboys, and Buckaroos.* Austin, Tex.: University of Texas Press, 2001.

On the Internet

The American West: Native Americans
www.americanwest.com/pages/indians.htm

Buffalo Bill's Wild West Show
www.buffalobill.com

Old West Gunfighters
www.legendsofamerica.com/we-gunfighterindex-a-b.html

Spanish Missions in the West
www2.scholastic.com/browse/article.jsp?id=5032

The websites listed on this page were active at the time of publication. The publisher is not responsible for websites that have changed their address or discontinued operation since the date of publication. The publisher will review and update the websites upon each reprint.

Index

Picture Credits

About the Author and the Consultant

Kenneth McIntosh is the author of more than sixty books, including titles in the Mason Crest series North American Indians Today. He also teaches college classes. He and his wife live in Flagstaff, Arizona, a town with an abundance of heritage sites from the 1800s.

John Gillis is a Rutgers University Professor of History Emeritus. A graduate of Amherst College and Stanford University, he has taught at Stanford, Princeton, University of California at Berkeley, as well as Rutgers. Gillis is well known for his work in social history, including pioneering studies of age relations, marriage, and family. The author or editor of ten books, he has also been a fellow at both St. Antony's College, Oxford, and Clare Hall, Cambridge.